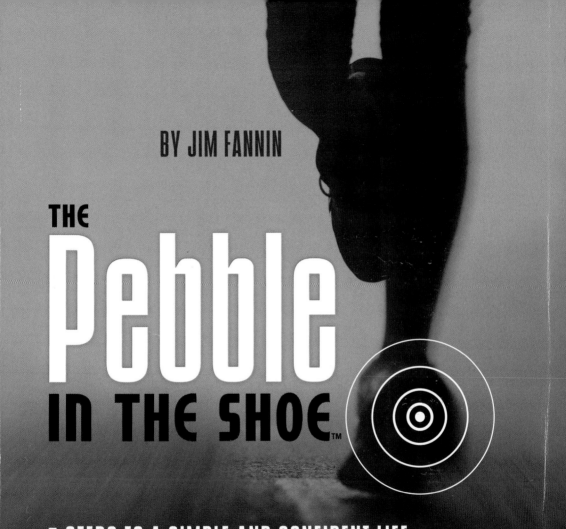

BY JIM FANNIN

THE Pebble
IN THE SHOE™

5 STEPS TO A SIMPLE AND CONFIDENT LIFE

Are YOU the *best* YOU can be?

THERE is one thing for sure in your life. Twelve months from now you will either be better or worse. You won't be the same. Will it be a roller-coaster ride to what you want, will it be two steps forward and one step back, or will you just go straight to your goals and visions? What's holding you back from business success, marital bliss or parenting nirvana? More than likely it's under the radar or below the surface of what you think. **Maybe, it's like a pebble in your shoe that's irritating, uncomfortable, nagging and eventually crippling.**

Today, through a simple story, you'll learn how a seemingly undetectable pebble can stop you from achieving your fullest potential. But, more importantly, you'll learn how to permanently remove those pebbles, making you able to approach any condition, circumstance or situation with confidence.

The
GREAT Race

All of the shoes stopped in front of the gates in anticipation of the GREAT RACE. From every corner of the land, thousands of pairs of footwear had independently marched to the stadium.

They had arrived at different times and soon would enter the massive structure together. A whispered buzz of excitement circled the vast array of shoes as they anxiously awaited to witness greatness.

Some shoes were very expensive Italian leather. Others were suede. Many were canvas. There were tennis shoes, soccer shoes, boots, pumps, loafers and even platforms. Some were knock-off brands and some were the real deal.

Only a few were ladies' high heels. You know…the real fancy kind. The shoes came in all colors, shapes and sizes. Some were scuffed up while others were shined military style. Many were new while others were old and worn out. Strangely, the higher quality shoes were lined up together. Designer shoes with designer shoes and discount shoes with their bargain basement buddies.

As the gates opened to the massive edifice, the shoes marched in organized chaos into the cavernous arena. Swiftly they found their seats.

SOON THE GREAT RACE WOULD BEGIN TO DETERMINE THE FASTEST IN THE LAND.

Although the shoes were different, they possessed three common denominators. First, they arrived as pairs. Second, all awaited the Great Race. And third, almost every pair held a foreign object and it wasn't just toes.

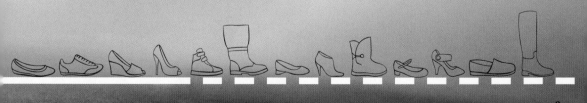

Tucked inside, between the feet and the soles, invisible tiny grains of sand were hiding. Over time many had grown into invisible pebbles. You couldn't see them but you could feel their nagging presence. One itsy, teeny, tiny stone hid undetected in a left shoe. Two microscopic ones nestled in the heel of a right-footed loafer. There were grains of sand and pebbles everywhere…hidden for no one to openly see. Only a few pair had none, at least for now.

The sun was bright and the mood of all the shoes was cheerful and hopeful. All thoughts were on the main event of the year, the running of the Great Race. Each foot tapped anxiously with the anticipation of the upcoming performance. Today they walked into the arena to watch the Champion and the contenders run. It was the foot race of all races.

GOLDEN SHOES

IT WAS THE GREAT RACE!

The winning shoes would be the fastest in the land. Each spectator had his or her favorite. But there was one pair that stood above the rest. Trimmed in gold with handcrafted, winged etchings, this amazing shoe moved onto the track with style and grace. Yes…the Champion has arrived. As the stadium shoes stomped in unison, the Golden Shoes kicked up his heels and the place went wild.

Who would win the race of the decade?
There were many "wannabes" that would love the coveted crown. Each had their logo of choice on the side of their shoe but none as distinct as the Champion. Most had no chance. At least that's what they thought and the crowd was in agreement. Would the competition wilt to the almighty pressure of the proven one? Probably. Even more than winning, how the golden pair would perform could determine the all-time record. This thought of a world record grasped the crowd with anticipated awe.

He was a champion runner. He had run this race before and he knew the competition well. He always beat them. He had never lost and he knew this race

would be no different. **In his mind, victory was sure.** He was the Golden Shoes.

A vapor cloud of suspense enveloped the thousands of shoes that gathered nervously to watch. Finally, a hush calmed the crowd as the runners gathered near the start. Each contestant began his last minute pre-race routine. Some were quiet. Others fidgeted and moved around. A few engaged with each other. One preened while another kept alone. A couple of shoes paced back and forth. Most believed they were ready. The Champion was steadfast with steely resolve. He was calm and cool as he thought,

"I AM THE CHAMPION!
I AM THE GOLDEN SHOES!"

Seconds before the starter's gun exploded, the Champion became concerned. "What's this?" he wondered. This had never happened. It was so small. It might have seemed insignificant to most. The enormous crowd of shoes hadn't noticed. The other competitors were unaware. The Champion felt the tiniest pebble in his shoe. **"On your mark!"** The stone was so miniscule. "Get set!" His energy gathered near the toe of his shoe. No longer was his focus piercing the track to the finish line.

"GO!"

With the earsplitting sound of the starter's gun, the Golden Shoes left the starting blocks with blinding speed, champion's speed. "I'm okay," he quickly thought. Now in full stride he could feel the intrusion of the stone and with each step the stone grew. He battled the obstruction while thoughts of doubt pierced his supremely confident mind. His once beautiful gait showcased a noticeable limp. He took his mind off of the finish line for the first time in his career. **And the crowd immediately knew something was wrong…terribly wrong.** They let out a "gasp" as the other contestants seemed to pick up the pace.

The Champion now could see his competitors from behind. They raced ahead into a blur of multi-colors that blocked the finish line from his view. One glanced back before confidently turning forward. Stunned by this

unfortunate circumstance, the Champion slowed to an average runner's pace. Today he would lose. How could something so small throw the Champion off course? How could something so tiny hobble the best in the land?

Golden Shoes was always free when he ran. Appearing to glide above the track as if he had wings, he moved effortlessly. **He was perfection to all that watched.** Nothing ever bothered him because he seldom ventured into the past and he rarely thought about the future. His domain was the present where champions reside. He had no equal. No peer. Built for speed, daring and panache, he was the Champion everyone looked up to and wanted to be. There were songs about him. He was showcased on billboards that lined the streets. Everything he did and said was watched and heard. He had been placed on a pedestal reserved only for greatness and he was admired, revered and imitated across the land.

Even as the eventual winner crossed the finish line, the victory seemed hollow. Something was wrong. Today, the mighty Champion would become a victim and he immediately blamed the pebble in his shoe. His mighty ego could not handle the responsibility. Even though he knew excuses were for losers, he bellowed, "I couldn't run. I had a pebble in my shoe." The other competitors were shocked at his reaction to losing. **"He is normal and not a god,"** a few thought. On this day Golden Shoes was a loser. The Champion did not prevail. He dropped his head for the first time and walked briskly into the bowels of the arena to quickly escape the crowd while they dispersed.

He has a PEBBLE IN HIS SHOE!

A SINGLE THOUGHT CAN REVERSE THE OUTCOME OF ANY SITUATION, CONDITION OR CIRCUMSTANCE.

What is your pebble?

EVERYONE has had a pebble in his or her shoe. You may have one or two now. It's the small, nagging thoughts that eventually weigh you down. Some pebbles have been hidden, undetected for years. Others push, prod, and make their presence felt every day. Each pebble intrudes into the lives of the unsuspecting. At different times in life the pebbles arrive. Although they are small and mostly undetected, they represent many unresolved thoughts, images and experiences. Some are pebbles of doubt. They form from a single thought that occurred years, months or weeks before. Some pebbles are lodged only in your business shoes. Some reside in your house slippers that you tuck under your bed. Some pebbles find their way

into your golf shoes while others form in the shoes worn while you parent. **Unfortunately, some pebbles travel in all your shoes regardless of where you walk or run.** Some pebbles are of fear. Others are created from guilt, rejection or shame. Maybe not today, but they eventually arrive unannounced and usually at the most inappropriate time. What challenges do they present?

To run the marathon race of life at your most efficient speed, you must be free of embarrassment, guilt, rejection, fear, envy, jealousy, anger, impatience, frustration and worry. All can be lodged in any shoe, from a pair of loafers worn by a city dweller in Manhattan, to a pair of boots on a farm in Montana. These intangible pebbles are crippling. They destroy relationships. They contribute to overeating

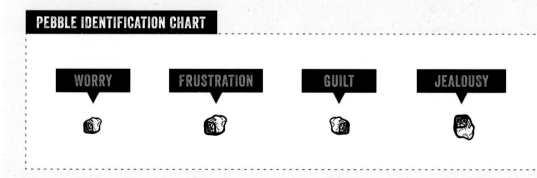

PEBBLE IDENTIFICATION CHART

WORRY   FRUSTRATION   GUILT   JEALOUSY

and gaining unhealthy weight. They coax us into drugs, alcohol and other addictions. They destroy families and alienate friends. They thwart the potential of our children and physically snuff extra years from our life. These are the pebbles in the shoe.

The pebble can cause you to quit or perform with complete indifference. It can help instigate a fight or add disrespectful silence to an otherwise dynamic relationship. Even the desire for fame, fortune or power can turn into a pebble in your shoe if left undetected. Most pebbles stir up the past, cloud the future and keep the present to a blink of the eye. Like a garden that's been freshly tilled, a pebble can reappear without warning or detection. **Prevention and removal are your only options for simplicity, balance and abundance.**

The
BUSINESS
Pebble

CONTENTS

Shoes of every kind filed out of the stadium in disbelief. They moved slowly in unison as if a funeral had let out. "Say it isn't so," the collective thought rang out. The questions bounced through the crowd seeking answers from no one in particular. "How could a champion of such stature lose because of a tiny pebble in his shoe?" asked a pair of flats. "Where did the pebble come from?" questioned a red pair of pumps. "I thought pebbles were only for ordinary shoes, not the Champion," queried the brown loafers. **"He makes so much money, why would he have issues like a tiny pebble?"** asked the blue sneakers.

An exquisite pair of black alligator loafers shuffled out of the arena in a hurry. "With the Great Race over, it's back to business. Sales have never been slower," he thought. Yes, he was successful. With no investors, he had worked from humble beginnings to factory owner of a 40,000-square-foot enterprise. But now his thoughts turned to making money. He didn't want money. He needed it.

"IF THE CHAMPION CAN STUMBLE BECAUSE OF A SMALL PEBBLE, THEN I AM VULNERABLE,"

he pondered silently to himself.

Inventory was over-flowing from the lack of new contracts. With suppliers and other creditors calling every day for payments, these factory owner shoes had become worn from pacing the vast floor. Over and over they would manically walk back and forth going nowhere.

WORRY

He had been living large. Expensive cars, houses and boats had all felt his black alligator loafers as they walked the insides of luxury. A lion doesn't hunt when its belly is full and this business lion got fat and lazy.

A pebble of worry now appeared. Worry that the sales of his products would not and could not overcome the volume of bills that were stacking up in his office. This nugget of minute-by-minute concern was beginning to hobble this formerly overconfident owner's strut. As he arrived home to his family, he walked by them as if they weren't there. Worry and stress has overcome reason and blinded this businessman to what really matters.

He has a PEBBLE IN HIS SHOE.

TURN YOUR TROUBLES INTO MOTIVATING CHALLENGES.

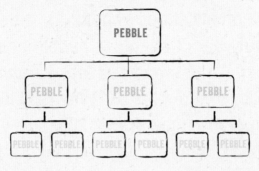

Pebbles of *negativity*

can impregnate a business or company with the speed of a computer virus.

TYPICALLY the pebbles form at the top where leadership resides. Eventually they will flow down through the management layers into the mindset of all employed. When every co-worker has a pebble or pebbles in their shoe, even the icons of industry can wither and die. They slow down the exceptional athlete or team and dramatically discourage the average among us. Even entire communities are not immune.

In the inner confines of the stadium the dejected Champion took off his shoes of gold. As street shoes became his footwear of choice, a pebble of a different kind showed up. As he stood and looked in the mirror, his heart sank as to thoughts of **"Why was the pebble in my shoe? How did it get there? What now?"**

For years the Champion was perfect. His wife and children were treated as royalty. Every pair of shoes wanted to get a glimpse of the Golden Shoes. Recently, he had slowed down his training. Overconfidence, coupled with unimagined fame, was an everyday thing. His wife complained he was not taking his training seriously. He was getting complacent and she warned him repeatedly. He felt she didn't believe in him. Her concerns seemed like nagging and they sparked daily arguments that were accelerating at an alarming rate. Shared vision was a thing of the past as they began going their separate ways.

Putting on a happy front in public was finally taking its toll with smiles turning to frowns when they were behind closed doors. Their children were photographed daily and abnormal living was their new normal as they could never escape the bright lights of fame. However, on this day, his wife and kids didn't even show up for the Great Race. Luckily, they didn't have to witness the Golden Shoes' demise.

Leaving the arena a fallen warrior will be this champion's most difficult time. Blame, guilt, embarrassment, panic and fear were now quickly forming more tiny pebbles in the shoes of the defeated great one. **His once eloquent posture and decisive manner has been removed like a robe.** His sense of purpose seems no more. With the arena now dark and empty, he can still feel the pebble in his shoe.

CHANGE HOW YOU FEEL BY CHANGING HOW YOU THINK.

The *average* person has
2,000 to 3,000
thoughts per day.

ON THE DAYS where life seems out of control and the "tail is wagging the dog," you may have 4,000 thoughts. Most thoughts are about the past. However, a great proportion of them are focused on the future. You cannot hold a future and a past-tense thought at the same time. It is one or the other. And a few thoughts are locked-in the moment. As you get older, present tense thinking diminishes. Throw in the cell phone, voicemails, e-mails, Tweets, Facebook, texts, FedEx, fax and world news in real time, it's no wonder present-tense living is dwindling.

Most pebbles originate from the past, with all of them negative. You can have experiences as far back as childhood that still tiptoe into your subconscious mind. They can even penetrate the consciousness of our daily actions. Over and over, we can play past tense thoughts that weigh negatively on our mind. They begin so innocently. Some are based on fact while other thoughts are based on assumption. Some are not true at all. Most are based on fear.

You have either positive or negative thoughts, but you can't think them at the same time. And the best news of all is you have free will to have any thought you choose. However, some negative thoughts can creep into your mind like a pebble in your shoe.

LIKE A PUPPETEER, YOUR

THOUGHTS

PULL THE STRINGS

OF ALL YOUR ACTIONS.

The PARENTAL Pebble

A teenage pair of tennis shoes skipped out of the arena very aware of how the Champion might be feeling. "He choked," thought the child prodigy golfer. Many tournament trophies line the shelves of this young athlete. The Great Race was an escape from his daily practice sessions and tournament play with his father overseeing every detail.

"KEEP YOUR HEAD STILL,"
THE PATRIARCH WOULD YELL.
"ARE YOU KIDDING ME?"

dear old Dad mumbles in the crowd as the "can't miss pro" missed another three-foot putt.

Within weeks, the teenage golf "phenom" would tee it up in the National Championships. **All eyes would point to his every move with two in particular watching with scrutiny and judgment.** After every swing or putt, the teenager will probably look to the side of the fairway or green to witness the body language of the man he loves. Some shots will undoubtedly cause an opened-mouth gasp while others will create joy and elation. During the

round, his Dad will cross his arms in disgust too many times to remember. And how about the car ride home? For years, lectures, inquisitions and silence have filled the auto interior as Dad sped down the highway from the golf course. "I hate it when he clams up and doesn't say a word. Those rides are the worst," the teenager thought. Guaranteed there will be a reaction from his father next week with every move he makes or doesn't make.

The young golfer swiftly runs ahead of the crowd. All alone he lets out a sigh as to how the Champion is feeling. He drops his head. He knows.

He has a PEBBLE IN HIS SHOE.

GREAT PARENTS LEVERAGE THE POSITIVES OF THEIR CHILDREN.

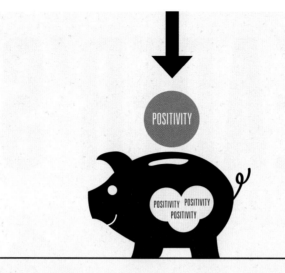

CONFIDENCE, TRUST, PRIDE AND POSITIVE SELF-ESTEEM
are all needed to be *the best* you can be.

A PEBBLE in the shoe can easily make withdrawals from your optimistic bank account. Champions know this and work daily to make deposits of positivity so their bank account is always full.

The **LEADER'S** Pebble

An extremely talented pair of ladies' red-bottomed shoes walked with poise into the street as she left the stadium. She's an aspiring corporate leader. **She has worked her way up the corporate ladder** and she's pushing against the glass ceiling of the male dominant leadership team. On the verge of being offered a seat at the C-suite table, the spotlight is bright and focused on this corporate climber. What's holding her back?

SHE'S BEEN SO BOLD UNTIL NOW.

The "moment of truth," when all in the company are watching her every move, has arrived. **"Grab the reins," screams her inner voice.**

"BUT, I WILL BE THE FIRST FEMALE CEO IN THE HISTORY OF THE COMPANY. HOW WILL THEY TREAT ME? WILL THEY LISTEN TO MY OPINIONS? WILL THEY TAKE ME SERIOUSLY? HOW CAN I BE ONE OF THE BOYS?"

She just got a pebble in her shoe. Has it been there all along? Probably.

It was in the fourth grade years ago when her father left home and abandoned her family. She felt it was her fault. At about the same time, he had refused to take her to the try-outs for the school play. This rejection by her father to let her participate in her "dream" activity was devastating. **"He makes me so mad. Why is he doing this to me? He must truly hate me. I know he's leaving us because of me."**

She eventually abandoned her childhood acting dream and chose a career path that she thought would make her business-mogul Daddy proud. From the best business school in the land to the top of her law school, she studied hard to enter and excel in corporate America. What's happening now that the grand prize has arrived? Is she afraid of failure? Is she afraid of rejection? Pressure can create a diamond over time but it can equally crush the meek and faint of heart. This extremely talented pair of ladies' red-bottomed shoes is starting to pull up at the finish line.

She has a PEBBLE IN HER SHOE.

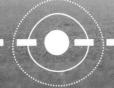

TAKE DOWN THE SAFETY NET OF LIFE AND GET UP ON THE HIGH WIRE WHERE ABUNDANCE AWAITS.

THE BEST in the world in any specific endeavor have a positive vision that wakes them up in the morning and tucks them into bed at night. With this vision of what they want indelibly etched in their minds, they mentally win first before they enter any performance. Now they are prepared to adjust or adapt to the ever-changing conditions, circumstances and situations they'll encounter. The rest enter the performance unprepared and then, and only then try to figure out what to do.

The SOCIAL Pebble

A pair of men's discreet dress shoes jumped ahead of the crowd trying to beat the traffic from the arena. **He came alone and would finally find solace in the darkness of his home.** He seldom ventured out with a group. He didn't date. He is a salesman by day and a social loner by night. The pebble in his shoe has been there for years.

"She is so beautiful," he thought a decade ago. After asking her to the dance, she blurted out in front of all his friends, **"No way would I go with you. Are you crazy?"**

This rejection was real. And even though it happened in high school, it formed a pebble in the shoe to cripple his social life. Ten years later, these shoes never set foot in front of a stylish pump. They would never approach even a cute pair of flats. Never! Are you kidding? He is still shy around ladies' footwear. Fear of rejection has lingered for years. It's even impacted many of his cold-call sales with the chemical company where he's employed. "How in the world did I become a salesman?" he thought. He always hits his quota but nothing more. He crumbles when the big money is on the table.

He has a PEBBLE IN HIS SHOE.

LAY DOWN
YOUR PROBLEM AND
PICK UP
THE CHALLENGE.

The CHAMPION'S
Pebble

After spending hours of solitude and deep introspection, the Champion finally began his short trek for home. **For the first time in his life, his post-race thoughts were about his family.** In the recent past, he had missed his daughter's piano recital due to a sponsor function. He had also missed his wedding anniversary when he ran a charity race out of the country. Even when he was home, he was not mentally there. All thoughts were on Golden Shoes. His life had been totally out of balance. The

miniscule pebble of guilt had grown over the past few months. A boulder was forming and life as he knew it was about to unravel faster than his sprinter's speed.

The Champion had taken himself too seriously. **All of his waking thoughts were spent on setting records.** Yes, he was great. Yes, his family lived a lavish, privileged life. But where was the shared family vision? Where was the family unity? What were his family's individual goals? In this life arena, he had no answers.

On this dismal night, he missed his wife and children. **Guilt had finally stopped his march to greatness.** Placing all of his happy eggs into the "Great Race" basket was a mistake. Finally he realized he was more than a champion sprinter. He was a father. He was a husband. Home never seemed so important as it did now. "I miss my family," he thought as he finally reached his doorstep. With all his family members asleep, he quietly found refuge in his bed. With his final thought of

"I LOST THE GREAT RACE BUT I REFUSE TO LOSE MY FAMILY,"

he envisioned unity and togetherness as he drifted off into the unknown future of a deep sleep.

SHARED VISION BROUGHT YOU TOGETHER.
SHARED VISION
WILL KEEP YOU TOGETHER.

DON'T LET YOUR PEBBLES BECOME BOULDERS

As you read this, place your attention
away from the book and *to* your shoes.

Any pebbles?

WHAT recurring thought or thoughts ricochet in your mind creating havoc and chaos in your decision-making? What dreams have you put on hold? Did the pebble in your shoe apply the brakes? Which pair of shoes has the pebble entered or has the pebble entered them all? Do not take your mind for granted. Like a pebble in a shoe, thoughts of worry, doubt and fear can grow to cripple your best intentions. It can stop you in your tracks. These tiniest of thoughts

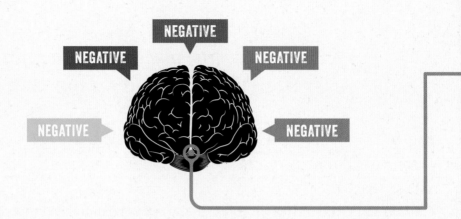

can manifest into major obstructions in your relationships and career. It's time to think about what you think about.

How did the pebbles get there? Thoughts from your past that linger will soon manifest themselves into reality. They can only grow if they're repeated or imagined over and over. "I can't believe she said that to me." And a few minutes later it is repeated, "I can't believe she said that to me." Throughout the day, this instant replay bounces off your mind like a pinball careening inside a glass case. This especially occurs when you think about what you DON'T want in your life.

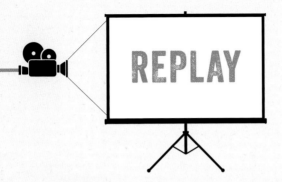

The next stage of pebble building occurs when you utilize your imagination and sprinkle it on the negative replay like seasoning from the kitchen cabinet. Now you project a thought or collection of thoughts into the future as in, "I bet she's seeing her ex-husband again. That's why she said those words to me." Of course, this make-believe scenario will ultimately cause a psychological car wreck to happen and the avoidable wreckage won't be pretty.

Carrying these tiny pebbles of doubt, rejection, guilt, embarrassment, jealousy, frustration, hopelessness and fear in your mind will soon find their way into your actions. In fact, negative thoughts left unattended most always turn into negative actions.

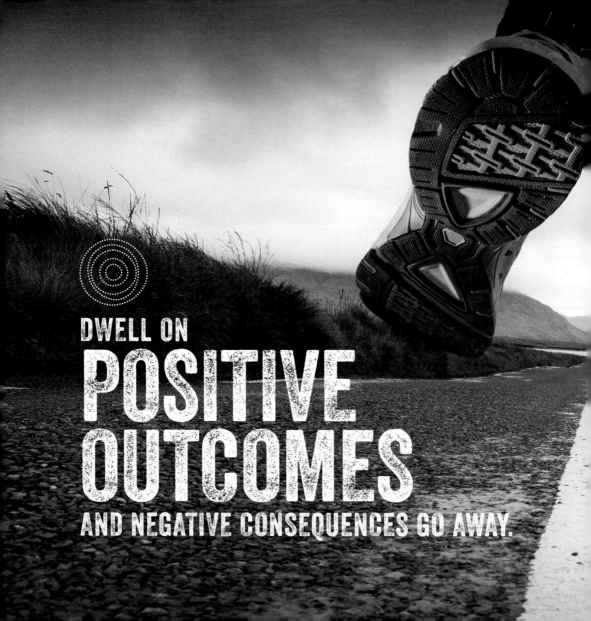

DWELL ON
POSITIVE
OUTCOMES
AND NEGATIVE CONSEQUENCES GO AWAY.

SEE WHAT YOU WANT:
NOT WHAT
YOU DON'T WANT

SUBCONSCIOUS DAILY RECORDING

HERE'S HOW the brain works for you and against you. Free will decides your fate. Every thought, feeling and sensation you have from the time you awake until you sleep at night is duly recorded by your subconscious mind and replayed 1 to 2 times once you are in a deep sleep or REM (rapid eye movement) state. The purpose of the replay is for storage. If the thought, feeling or sensation is important, it will be stored near the surface of your mind for easy access. If the thought, feeling or sensation is of little or no importance, it is stored or buried in the deepest recesses of your brain. The following, however, solidifies the pebble in the shoe.

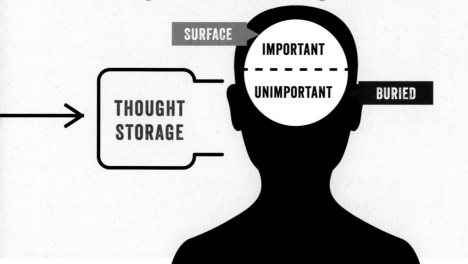

SURFACE

IMPORTANT

UNIMPORTANT

BURIED

THOUGHT STORAGE

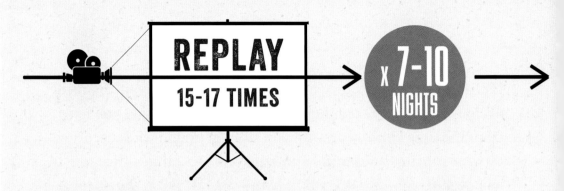

REPLAY
15-17 TIMES

x **7-10** NIGHTS

During the last 30 minutes prior to deep sleep, your thoughts, feelings and sensations are recorded just like the rest of your day. However, these thoughts are not only recorded, but they are replayed 15 to 17 times during your sleep. It is these particular thoughts that pack the biggest punch. That's right! After 7 to 10 nights of replaying the same thoughts, regardless if they are positive or negative, your subconscious mind believes this is what you want. And of course, you have free will so why wouldn't it think this? This repetition stresses your entire internal system. It activates your intuition and all of your powerful mental faculties. Now your subconscious will do everything in its power to manifest itself into its physical equivalent.

Repetitive thoughts before sleep over 7 to 10 successive nights will create synchronicity, coincidence and happenchance and other phenomenon to make it so, even if it's bad for you. I have personally

SYNCHRONICITY, COINCIDENCE AND HAPPENCHANCE

utilized visualization techniques for all my clients to help them rise from rags to riches or mediocrity to superstardom. Unfortunately, I witnessed many people experience the reverse because of their negativity. **It is this repetition that forms the pebble.**

Check your mind for the bothersome grains of indecision, uncertainty, chaos, hesitation, vagueness, ambiguity, insecurity and confusion. Clear the thoughts of what you don't want for the race ahead in life, business, relationships and family. **Run with purpose. Run fast when you can. Be careful on the curves and the steep terrain. Stop periodically to rest and enjoy the scenery. Then move ahead at your pace, free from the man-made pebbles of negativity.**

YOUR POSITIVE VISION NEEDS TO

WAKE
YOU UP

IN THE MORNING AND PUT YOU
TO SLEEP AT NIGHT.

HOW TO PERMANENTLY
REMOVE
YOUR PEBBLES

Preparation

is the hallmark of being the best you can be.

WORRY ANGER FEAR

PREPARATION

TRUST CONFIDENCE ADAPT

KNOWING that you are ready for any condition, circumstance or situation is a definite confidence builder. All champions feel they are the best prepared in the arena. They trust that what they have is enough. They are ready to adapt and adjust to the first sign of a pebble of negativity.

Here are five simple, champion-tested tools for removing the smallest to the largest pebble in your shoe. You will now be armed to combat all negative thoughts that may attempt to penetrate your mind. Of course, keeping your shoe free of the pebble is the ultimate quest.

The PALM TREE™

The palm tree reacts to a hurricane or violent storm by allowing the negativity to pass through it by bending with the violent winds.

IT absorbs the energy and the devastating wrath of the storm. After the hurricane dissipates and departs, the palm stands up straight to see another day of sunshine. It symbolizes all that's good about the sun, beach, ocean, recreation and pleasure.

An oak tree, of course, would brace itself and fight the 80 to 100 mph forces. It would fight with all of its strength to not succumb to the hurricane's fury. With a mighty, but futile attempt, it would be left with broken branches or tree trunk. Maybe it would be uprooted and scattered. This is why you never see oak trees on the beach.

Hurricanes of life are more frequent than the real ones that wreak havoc on our beaches. They arrive internally and externally into our lives. Some we create and others are cast upon us. Managing these negative forces depends on how you think during situations, conditions and circumstances of stress.

Here's how to manage the psychological hurricanes that arrive in your life. Within 90 seconds of receiving negative news, having a major disagreement, reality not meeting your expectations, abuse from a road-raged driver, being placed on hold by the utility company, or discovering any type of pebble, become the palm tree by doing the following:

1. **Unhinge your jaw**

2. **Lower your breathing to approximately 6 to 8 breaths per minute**

3. **Picture a palm tree in your mind.**

4. **Absorb the negativity and let it pass through you like the palm tree.**

5. **After the hurricane blows itself out, mentally see the outcome as you want.**

6. **Feel the sunshine on your face.**

7. **Regularly remind yourself of the Palm Tree when there's a pebble in your shoe.**

Now you know the Palm Tree and you'll be ready when a life hurricane arrives. When the negative winds from situations, conditions or circumstances become apparent, you'll become relaxed, poised and peaceful. This will take practice and preparation, as surprise will certainly catch you off guard.

BUT WHAT IF the hurricane has originated from your pebble and not the pebble in the shoe from someone else?

When you were a young child many conditions, circumstances and situations had a major impact on how you think and react. Some of these occurrences created pebbles that could easily trigger small hurricanes on unsuspecting friends, family and even strangers. This can cause mild to severe reactions.

My father seldom lost his temper. However, if he were told point blank that he couldn't do something, he would throw a fit. His face would contort and he'd begin to chew on the tiny flap of skin on the inside corner of his mouth that was reserved for "chewing when upset." My mother learned over time to steer clear of this potential hurricane. This was a pebble in my father's shoe. Over time, he figured out how to remove this part of him that contributed to many actions that he regretted.

Recently, I've noticed more and more people getting upset if their expectations of what they want don't match the reality of what they received. Many people have been acting like this since childhood. Many teenagers (maybe you have one living in your house) are just starting to take this to another level. It has become the pebble in their shoe. Not getting your way can lead to many emotions and eventual anger. In fact, anger is never the first emotion. You will experience jealousy, impatience, frustration, embarrassment, envy and eventually anger.

WHAT EXTERNAL STATEMENTS, acts or situations jostle the pebble in your shoe and conjure up the dormant hurricane forces inside you?

Know them. They are warning you and eventually warning others within your proximity. Some of the signals are tightness in the chest, clenched jaw and fists, piercing eyes, furrowed brow, shortness of breath and crossed arms. Be aware of the internal warning winds of negativity. You have free will on how to respond and react. Don't forget.

Keep the image of the palm tree in your mind and at the ready. Be armed when the time comes to utilize its services. Be aware of your thoughts and feelings **and you will control your actions and ultimately the pebble in your shoe.**

*The exquisite pair of black alligator loafers of the **factory owner** had an epiphany. First, he realized he'd become fat and lazy with success. And finally, he panicked and became stressed at an economy that's impacted everyone, not just his company.*

*In this financial hurricane, he has finally adopted the mindset of **the Palm Tree**. In fact, every co-worker in the factory has received a "Palm Tree" button to wear. Several live palm trees have been brought onto the factory floor and a giant palm tree has been placed in the corporate office rotunda. He is now energized after discovering he was only thinking what he didn't want in his life and business. He had become stressed by internalizing his problems. In fact, the word "problem" has been removed from his vocabulary as well. He has replaced it with the word*

"challenge" which has energized everyone in the company. He and his employees have become palm trees in this economic hurricane. And now when he goes home, he's fully engaged with the ones he loves.

THE PALM TREE
removed the pebble in his shoe.

BE THE "PALM TREE" IN ALL OF LIFE'S HURRICANES.

The LIGHT SWITCH™

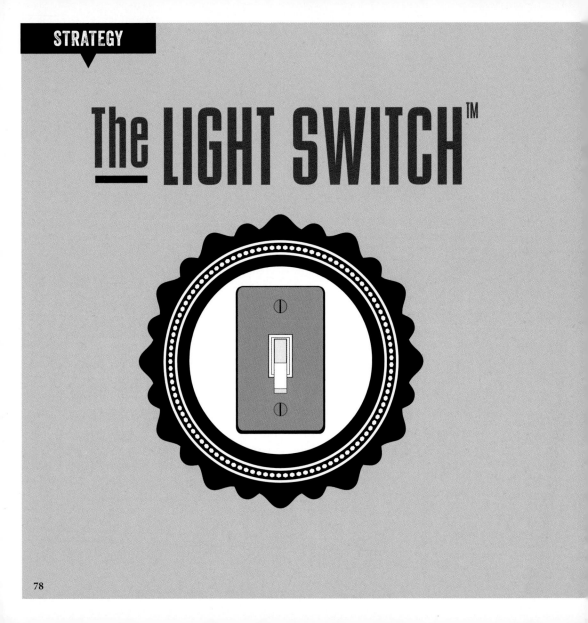

Like a light switch on the wall, your head can move up and down and vice versa.

IN fact, it operates literally like a light switch in many ways. When the switch is placed in the up position, the light goes on and your surroundings are bright. When the switch is in the down position, the light is turned off and the surrounding area is dark. Your brain is no different. Here's how:

Right now, I want you to do something I will never ask you to do again. First, shut your eyes. Now I want you to place a negative image in your mind. Hold that thought. Next, I want you to put your head down on your chest or your sternum. Drop your head and hold the negative thought. Make it real. Make it vivid. I want you to see and feel whatever you're thinking.

Now, with the same negative thought, raise your head up, above the parallel point. Put your chin up high and see if you can hold that same negative thought. With the negative thought still in your mind, drop your head again. Continue to raise and lower your head like a light switch being turned on and off several more times while maintaining the negative thought.

Over a million attendees at my seminars and speeches throughout my career experienced the following. See for yourself. **With the chin up above the parallel point, more than 80 percent of those trying this exercise had a difficult time keeping the negative thought clear in their mind.** In fact, most had to recreate it or conjure it back into their consciousness. However, with the head down, negatives rushed into the brain with incredible clarity.

To remove and keep out the pebble in your shoe, we need to make a rule right here, right now.

"Dropping your head is <u>NOT</u> an option." I repeat, "Dropping your head is <u>NOT</u> an option."

It's not acceptable—especially when something doesn't go your way. Mom was right. Keep your chin up!

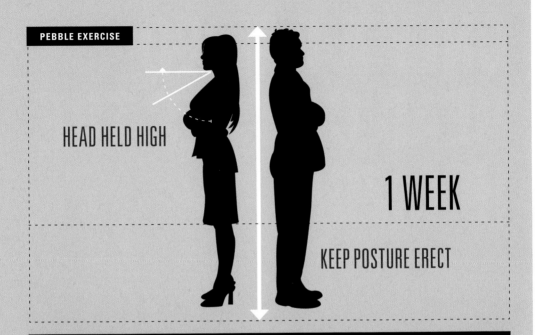

HEAD HELD HIGH

1 WEEK

KEEP POSTURE ERECT

Your exercise over the next week is to walk with your posture erect and your head held high. See how you feel at the end of the day. I'll bet that you are more positive, upbeat, and confident, thus increasing your optimism level. And if you discover a pebble in your shoe, raise your head high and replace the negative thought with something that you want instead of don't want. Use the Light Switch.

ONLY A RAISED HEAD CAN SEE THE HORIZON.

The salesman woke up a new man. After exchanging his men's discreet dress shoes for a pair of chic black Italian loafers, he had committed to total positivity. **On every sales call today he pledged to keep his chin up regardless of the acceptance or rejection from the prospective client.** Cold call after cold call his head remained high. By noon he couldn't believe that not one negative thought entered his mind. At one stop there was a terse rejection that had typically flattened his ego, but not today. Nothing entered his mind but the satisfaction of seeing his "new" customer reap the benefits of his products and services.

With a revitalized outlook he made one of the biggest decisions of his life. Celebration at a trendy restaurant/ bar would be his reward for an awesome day. Nice. Confidently, with chin up and the Light Switch on, he walked into the dark lit room to a group of strangers.

He smiled to a beautiful pair of red pumps. Later that evening he approached a pair of burgundy platform court shoes, some fancy peep-toe, sling-back sandals, and a chic pair of black, studded flats. "Wow! Where have I been?" he thought as his confidence permeated the room.

THE LIGHT SWITCH is on.

The REBOOT™

3

IF a pebble in your shoe has revealed itself, use the tool called the Reboot. Your conscious mind can easily become cluttered and over-loaded. It's no different than a computer that has too many programs open and too many items on the desktop. What happens to your computer? It can slow down or even freeze. Your brain is the same. What do you do? You don't pop out the motherboard and fix it. You

Reboot. Your brain works the same way. And there are two ways to use the Reboot tool. One is before you begin any life, business or sports performance and the other is after the performance is under way.

Before you conduct or enter a meeting, take an exam, play a round of golf, begin a negotiation, initiate a sales call, or any other important performance, clear your mind with the Reboot. Here's how it works.

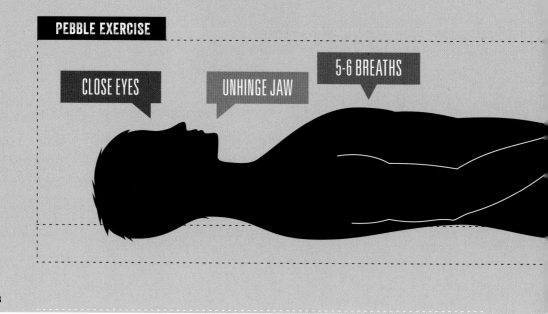

PEBBLE EXERCISE

CLOSE EYES

UNHINGE JAW

5-6 BREATHS

Close the door on what you've been doing. Get into the moment by shutting your eyes and relaxing them. Unhinge your jaw. Take five or six deep breaths. Turn your mind off and be still (lying down is preferable, if possible) for 90 seconds. See a blank or black screen in your mind. Detach yourself from the outcome of the performance. Be in the moment in your stillness. After nearly two minutes of silence, open your eyes and raise your chin slightly above parallel.

You have now rebooted your brain from past-tense thoughts,

EXERCISE DURATION: **90** SECONDS

and other negatives. You've cleared the mental clutter and surrendered to your amazing subconscious mind. With a clear mind, you are now prepared to send your energy to the opening task at hand. Now with full engagement, enter the next arena confident and ready to go.

During any performance, negativity can sneak into your mind. The pebble can begin to protrude into the moment. What do you do? Reboot. It's the same tool but it now needs less time to execute. In fact, every athlete I've coached has used the Reboot in some of the most pressure-packed moments like the Masters, World Series, and the Super Bowl. It's even been used before a multi-national annual shareholders meeting, major acquisition negotiation and the Academy Awards show. Some of my professional golf clients may reboot 10 to 15 times during a round. The Reboot will last only a few seconds. The longest you would need to Reboot would be 30 seconds. That should get your computer brain restarted and refocused on the task at hand.

In addition, the Reboot is a great tool to assist you in prolonging the purposeful calm mindset athletes and peak performers call the Zone. This is where you are at your best. If things are going well and you become aware of being in the Zone, then Reboot. There have been 16 Major League Baseball players that hit four home runs in one game. Two of them were my clients and each rebooted multiple times to keep their minds from over-thinking the situation. This action will assist you in stretching the time limit of the Zone mindset.

THE ZONE ● MINDSET

When you become aware of a pebble in your shoe, try the Reboot.

Now walking in black and white golf shoes the child prodigy golfer has already begun play in the National Golf Championships. A pre-performance Reboot cleared his mind from the past and helped him detach from the possible outcome. After three holes, an unfortunate errant tee shot careens off a cart path and barely stays in play. He knows his father's glare is there because he can feel it. **With a smile he Reboots and gathers his energy for his next target.** He flushes it on the green and this teenage whiz kid is now in total control of his thoughts.

   With a final 12-foot birdie putt that finds the bottom of the 18th cup, he raises his hands above his head in victory. Not once did he look to his father during the round. Not one time. As he walked off the green, his Dad hugged him and whispered, "You were a man today. I'm so proud of you. More importantly, I'm proud to be your father." They both cried and walked shoulder to shoulder to the clubhouse.

"YOU WERE A MAN TODAY.

**I'M SO PROUD OF YOU.
MORE IMPORTANTLY,
I'M PROUD TO BE
YOUR FATHER."**

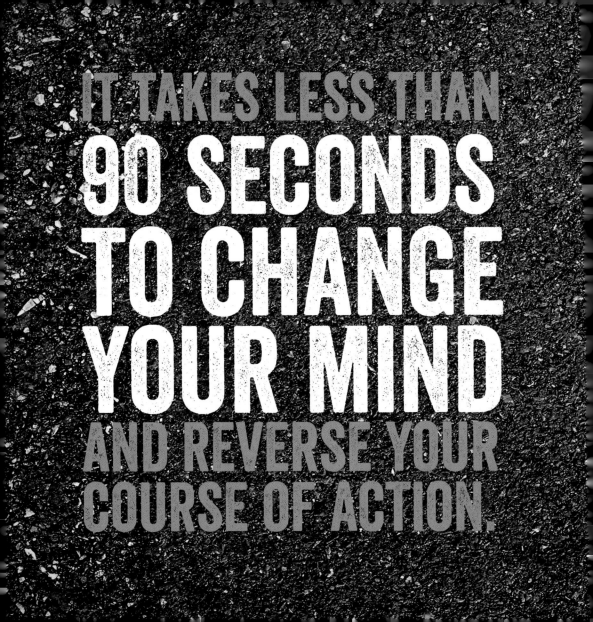

The MENTOR IMAGE™

4

When a negative thought occurs or a series of negativity has you cornered with no place to go, think the image of your mentor, loved one, coach, parent or religious figure.

IT will take your mind from the pebble in your shoe to where you want to go. This mental image will inspire you and help you overcome all obstacles and hardships.

Over 50 years ago, I walked to Central Park in Ashland, Kentucky, and was prepared to play tennis for the first time. I was 11 years old. My neighborhood friend had invited me to play and I had no clue about the etiquette or the rules of the game.

Upon arriving at the public courts, we reserved court #5 for an hour with the Director of Tennis, Professor R.W. Ross. The Professor was a 73-year-old African-American who taught YMCA tennis and

Jack Ditty, (Jim's state champions double partner) Professor R.W. Ross and Jim Fannin

scheduled the courts. Dressed in all white he moved with grace and his lean, muscular body was a reflection of his self-discipline.

It was 12:55 pm and our court was open even though our reservation wasn't scheduled until 1:00 pm. I quickly bolted through the gates and sprinted behind courts #3 and #4 as the "Prof" yelled,

"STOP! Come back here, right now!"

I remember freezing as his words pierced through the air and found its mark.

"Yes sir," I said. He then proceeded to tell me the proper etiquette was to never walk or run behind someone's court while the ball was in play. In addition, my court was at 1:00 pm and not 12:55 pm. As I waited, I witnessed everyone at the packed courts honoring these rules. Exactly on the hour, the Professor would blow a whistle and call out, "One o'clock! With his announcement the people on the courts either continued to play or they left. You could only reserve one hour for singles and two hours for doubles. Discipline was in the house. There was no profanity, horseplay or obnoxious behavior. No one argued. Everyone knew the rules and the proper conduct that was expected. And everyone knew who was in charge.

After I finished playing, the "Prof" advised I sign up for lessons. On his advice my tennis career had begun. And my coaching career would soon take root.

One year later, the Professor taught me how to teach the six-year-old kids in the beginner's program. The following year I taught more students and continued teaching under his guidance for 10 years until I graduated from college.

He told me once, before I played a tournament, to "come home with the trophy." It was not a kind gesture. It was an order. He said, **"What you have is enough to win."** With little money, one racket and no ride, I hitch-hiked from Ashland to Lexington, Kentucky. (Mom never found out;

please don't do this today). I won the tournament after hearing his words in my mind, "what you have is enough to win." Upon hitching a ride home 127 miles with the champion's trophy, I couldn't wait to show him the hardware.

I won the first professional tournament named in his honor some years later. With the "Prof" in the stands, I beat a Nigerian Davis Cup player that was better than me. With only a nod of quiet confidence from my mentor, I reached into my inner strength and overcame a seemingly unbeatable foe.

After encouragement from the "Prof," I won the Ohio Valley Conference Championships at East Tennessee State University by beating three players in a row that had all beaten me just weeks earlier.

He went with me in spirit as I played on the professional tour in Europe. Country to country, his wisdom followed me. Later, I coached seven players into the world's top 10 with information formed from my Central Park days in Ashland.

Years would go by and the words of the Professor would still echo in my mind. I thought of him often and still do. When a pebble was felt in my shoe and I would begin to falter or slow down, I thought of him. He was wise. He was quiet, yet so powerful. He was just. He was consistent. He was humble. He was tough, yet kind. How could a black man in Appalachia in the 1960s influence so many young white kids? How could he impact so many lives?

Here's just some of what I learned.

 When you commit to a time or schedule, honor it. Your word is your bond. "I was never late under the Professor's watch. Never."

 Outwork everyone. "I arrived before him and left at dark when he did for 10 years during the summers."

Know that one look or word can and probably does impact your students. As a teacher, you are constantly influencing thoughts. Your actions can last a lifetime. "I didn't realize it at the time. I thought I was just teaching tennis."

Lead by example. He did every day. I never heard or saw him angry, sad, impatient or even negative. Ever! "I've tried my best to emulate his ways."

Hold your students accountable. Not in a mean or too tough way, but in an "I care about you" way. "I do. Period!"

 Use catch phrases or themes that trigger mental images of what you want your students to learn. "Now you know where I get this."

 Use repetition to influence thoughts. Disguise it by saying the same thing in different ways. "This is an art form."

 See the positive and the potential in each student. Let this be your guiding light as they encounter challenges with each subject. "This was my special gift from him."

 Judiciously sprinkle praise on your students. Motivate and encourage them.

 Learn as well as teach, "Never, never, never give up." "I instilled this in my daughter and she has exemplified this maxim."

Visualization is one of the most powerful tools for teaching and learning. "This has been a daily tool for me for over 50 years."

 If you want someone to relax then you need to be relaxed yourself. "I am the palm tree."

 Respect your opponent by beating them as badly as possible. Cut them no slack. "The 'Prof' pounded this into all of us."

 Challenge your students to be the best they can be. "Seeing my students meet my challenge gives me my greatest pleasure."

 Be prepared. Dress rehearse everything. "I envisioned this book well before it was written. In fact, I've never had a day I haven't already had. Thanks Prof."

Not that long ago I drove over 400 miles to Ashland, Kentucky, where my mentor, Professor R.W. Ross was being posthumously inducted into the Kentucky Tennis Hall of Fame. If he had been alive, he would have been 123 years old. The Ross family of son, daughter, grandchildren, and great grandchildren flew in from all across the country. The son, Washington Dubois Ross, was at the time 93-years old and was one of the last four, living Tuskegee Airmen from World War II. He was amazing. When I saw him walk into the venue, I thought he was the Professor.

I was the keynote speaker and closed the evening. Acorns don't fall far from the tree. There were many acorns there and I was one of them.

I loved the Professor. He loved me. I hope I grew to be the man he hoped I would be. His memory and positive mentor image has definitely helped me extract many pebbles from my shoe.

Who is your mentor image?

50 years later, Jack Ditty, Washington Dubois Ross and Jim Fannin

GREAT LEADERS BECOME WHAT THEY WANT THEIR FOLLOWERS TO BE.

An aspiring corporate leader stood in the hallway a few steps from the company boardroom. Many thoughts raced through her mind. Finally a pebble revealed itself. It has been there for years. Fear of success and the feelings of abandonment have formed over time. But not today! One image took over the movie screen of her mind. Mom. The one person taken for granted has been the rock that has made her the woman she is now. **Her mother took two jobs after her father left them in the middle of the night. She inspired her to go to college and eventually law school.** It was her mother's courage and capacity to look forward that gave her the motivation to be the best she could be.

As she saw her mother's face in her mind, the pebbles of doubt and fear went away. And with this mentor image, she replayed the words her mother spoke the night before, "Be the actress you've always wanted to be.

ACT AS THE LEADER YOUR COMPANY'S BEEN WAITING FOR."

With confidence the extremely talented pair of ladies' red-bottomed shoes walked into the boardroom of black, winged-tipped corporate clones. Poised and sure of herself she stood and addressed the current leadership team. Looking each man in the eye before she spoke she said, "Gentlemen, today our company is at a crossroad. Looking back on what's transpired is not an option. **I see the one clear path we can take to set us apart from the competition while leveraging our skillsets to capture more market share.** Open the folder in front of you and you'll find a strategy that will translate straight to the bottom line." A smile crossed the Founder/Chairman's face and the rest of the leadership team proceeded like lemmings to explore the company's new direction. Thanks Mom.

The Most Powerful FOUR-LETTER™ WORD

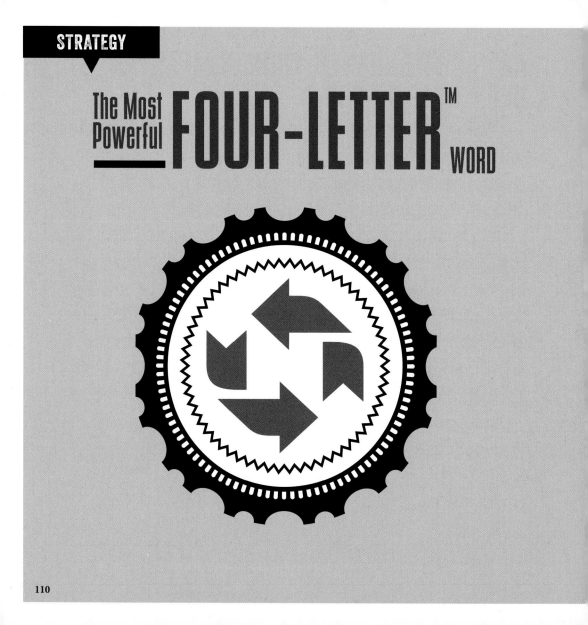

5

There is one word that will guide you to success. This small word will keep you moving forward.

IT will single-handedly extract the pebble in your shoe and remove you from negative situations, conditions and circumstances. What is this power word?

Obviously, the words love, belief, expectancy and faith come to the forefront as power words. The words of confidence, trust, knowing and self-discipline will all get some votes. I have probably said the word "awesome" over 150,000 times to my clients. I even say it to strangers as in "Awesome" as my reply to their "How are you?" But there is one, single word that stands out in my career as a coach, mentor, guide, trainer, educator and cheerleader.

What is the power word? What one word comes to your mind?

There is one word that has been said every day in my 40 years of coaching. This one word has been mentioned to every client in every situation, condition and circumstance. This powerful four-letter word keeps all of my clients grounded. It moves them inch-by-inch toward their vision and goals.

What is this power word? I say it when you've been your worst. I say it when you have performed in the peak performance mindset called the Zone and your best has surfaced.

I said this word just after one-armed baseball pitcher, Jim Abbott, hurled a no-hitter in Yankee stadium. I used this word after PGA superstar Luke Donald won his first 72-hole professional tournament. It was repeated multiple times when MLB All-Star Mike Cameron blasted four home runs in one game. This word has been used on CEOs, *New York Times* best-selling novelists, student athletes, parents struggling with their teenaged children, couples considering divorce, cancer patients and Olympic Gold Medalists.

This word can eliminate worry. If said with passion, conviction and positivity, it will catapult you from despair and thrust you into hope and possibility.

When you fail, this word needs to surface. When you get full of yourself, bring this word to the forefront. When you're lost, have it on your mind. Put it somewhere in your car. Write it on your bathroom mirror. Have this word permanently engraved in your brain. Carry it with you on the golf course. Think it after every errant shot. **Think it after every business meeting.** Think it after any crisis, confrontation or debacle.

When you're bogged down with challenges and there's a pebble in your shoe, think...

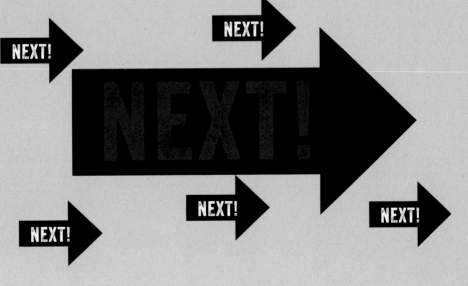

POSSIBILITY

POSSIBILITY

POSSIBILITY

POSSIBILITY

NEXT

Say it to yourself right now. NEXT! Say it with enthusiasm. Verbalize it with the feeling of excitement for what's in store for you. Use it only in a positive context. Try it again. **Raise the octave in your voice. NEXT!** The word "next" points you to the future. It becomes your compass for possibility. It closes the door on what just happened. It guides you toward a solution to your challenge. It shines a beacon of hope on your next step.

The word *Next* is the name of an album for the hall of fame group, Journey. It's a movie starring Nicholas Cage. It's the title of a play by Terrence McNally. It's the name of a music industry magazine and a

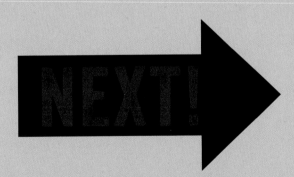

book title by Michael Crichton. It's the name of a well-known Indian electronics retailer. But it's more than a word. It's more than a name.

The great champions I've met and coached did three things that helped them become successful.

FIRST ▶ They only went into the past for swift analysis, evaluation and learning (the exception, of course, is the past has funny stories and experiences that we can share with friends).

SECOND ▶ These champions only went into the future for planning, strategy and tactics.

THIRD ▶ And most importantly, they performed in the moment or the "now" focusing only on their "next" move. The word "next" helped them manage this entire process. And the pebble in the shoe will be gone.

My family has been instructed to place this word somewhere on my tombstone. I'm not 100 percent positive what will happen to me after my brief stint on earth. But I know one thing is for sure…my mindset…my spirit…my soul…will approach the unknown with a passion for what lies ahead. And this word will be carried with me as I approach my future.

The smell of coffee, waffles, bacon and eggs permeated the Champion's darkened bedroom. "Hmmm…my favorite meal," he thought as he wiped the sleep from his eyes. With his memory from his all-night guilt-fest and hellish day at the track just beginning to resurface, he got up gingerly and shuffled to the kitchen. As he ate breakfast with his family, no one spoke a word. The Great Race was never mentioned. While his wife cleared the table, the Champion ambled to the bathroom to take a shower. As he looked at the husband, father and man in the mirror, he noticed a handwritten note from his wife that read:

SUCCESS IS GETTING UP ONE MORE TIME FROM DEFEAT. NEXT!

In the corner of the mirror, the reflection of the Golden Shoes protruded from his closet. He quickly found his wife, apologized for his mental disconnect and gave her an "I love you forever" embrace. "Thank you," he whispered. "You are my life." And with that he wiped a tear from his eye, laced up his Golden Shoes, and headed out the door for a run.

NEXT!

NEXT

**THIS IS THE BATTLE CRY
OF THE CHAMPION.**

Do *you* have a *pebble* in your shoe?

I'M SURE in the past you've limped into a few meetings, been off-balance in a couple of confrontations, or moved gingerly as you stepped into a difficult fairway bunker.

However, the next time you go to your closet to find your shoes, look at them with different eyes. Inspect each pair more closely. You have shoes for all occasions. You walk in them to work. You hike in a pair of boots that lie in the corner. You play golf in a few. You jog in a few. Each represents one of the multiple arenas of your life. When each shoe is worn, what thoughts dominate your mind?

Are you clear of all doubt, fear, worry, anxiety, jealousy, apathy, indecision or desperation?

Which pair, if any, has a pebble in the shoe? Remove it before your feet find the soles. Each time you put on a pair of shoes, see what you want from the arena you will enter next. Make up your mind that no thought of negativity will make its way into your thoughts. And if it happens, know you have solutions for handling the negative mental intrusion that can be so irritating, uncomfortable, nagging and eventually crippling.

As you walk among hundreds of shoes in the next few days, keep your head held high. Smile because you know your shoes are different from the rest. You've removed the pebble in the shoe and you're ready to blast it to dust if it ever returns.

Greatness is measured by the differential between your best and worst day.

JIM FANNIN is the "World's #1 Coach of Champions" by producing more champions in sports, business and life than anyone on earth since 1974. He is a mental performance coach, author, professional platform speaker, life strategist, sports & business consultant, and former professional tennis player. He has 35+ years of professional coaching, consulting and public speaking experience.

Mr. Fannin has privately coached hundreds of professional athletes from 10 sports with 25 MLB All-Stars (including 4 Cy Young Award winners, 6 MVPs and two batting champions), Olympic gold medalists, seven world's top-10 ranked professional tennis players (including a 4-time Wimbledon Doubles Champion, French Open Champion and Runner-up), NBA All-Stars, NFL All-Pros, MLS MVP and 10 golfers to win their first professional tournament.

In addition, Jim has personally trained tens of thousands of corporate executives and hundreds of companies from 50 industries in peak performance. From leadership teams and sales organizations, Jim's thought management systems have made an impact.

Due to the dramatic results from Jim's Golf in the Zone™ Schools, Life Seminars™, Leadership in Tough Times™ Retreats, Sales in the Zone™ Seminars, corporate keynotes, personal coaching and consulting, his services are in high demand. In addition, Jim has published multiple best-selling works including eight *In the Zone* audio products, *S.C.O.R.E.® for Life* book, and the internationally renowned *90 Second Rule*™ audio/DVD program.

For more information about Jim, to inquire about speaking engagements, or to learn more about incorporating *The Pebble in the Shoe* into your next event, visit www.jimfannin.com, call 877-210-2001 or email askjim@jimfannin.com.

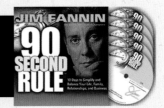

What OTHERS are saying...

We purchased a Simple Truths' gift book for our conference in Lisbon, Spain. We also personalized it with a note on the first page about valuing innovation. I've never had such positive feedback on any gift we've given. People just keep talking about how much they valued the book and how perfectly it tied back to our conference message.

— **Michael R. Marcey,** Efficient Capital Management, LLC.

The small inspirational books by Simple Truths are amazing magic! They spark my spirit and energize my soul.

— **Jeff Hughes,** United Airlines

Mr. Anderson, ever since a friend of mine sent me the 212° movie online, I have become a raving fan of Simple Truths. I love and appreciate the positive messages your products convey and I have found many ways to use them. Thank you for your vision.

— **Patrick Shaughnessy,** AVI Communications, Inc.

127